Collins

Reading Comprehension Progress Tests

Year 6 / P7

Author:
Stephanie Austwick

Series editors:
Stephanie Austwick
and Rachel Clarke

William Collins's dream of knowledge for all began with the publication of his first book in 1819.

A self-educated mill worker, he not only enriched millions of lives, but also founded a flourishing publishing house. Today, staying true to this spirit, Collins books are packed with inspiration, innovation and practical expertise. They place you at the centre of a world of possibility and give you exactly what you need to explore it.

Collins. Freedom to teach.

Published by Collins
An imprint of HarperCollins*Publishers*
The News Building
1 London Bridge Street
London
SE1 9GF

Browse the complete Collins catalogue at
www.collins.co.uk

© HarperCollins*Publishers* Limited 2019

10 9 8 7 6 5 4 3 2 1

ISBN 978-0-00-833348-5

British Library Cataloguing-in-Publication Data

A catalogue record for this publication is available from the British Library.

Author: Stephanie Austwick

Series editors: Rachel Clarke, Stephanie Austwick

Publisher: Katie Sergeant

Product Manager: Catherine Martin

Development editor: Judith Walters

Copyeditor and typesetter: Hugh Hillyard-Parker

Proofreader: Catherine Dakin

Cover designers: The Big Mountain

Production controller: Katharine Willard

Printed and bound by CPI Group (UK) Ltd, Croydon, CR0 4YY

MIX
Paper from
responsible sources
FSC www.fsc.org **FSC™ C007454**

This book is produced from independently certified FSC paper to ensure responsible forest management.

For more information visit: **www.harpercollins.co.uk/green**

The publishers gratefully acknowledge the permission granted to reproduce the copyright material in this book. Every effort has been made to trace copyright holders and to obtain their permission for the use of copyright material. The publishers will gladly receive any information enabling them to rectify any error or omission at the first opportunity.

TEXT

An extract on pp.7-8 from *The Weirdstone of Brisingamen* reprinted by permission of HarperCollins Publishers Ltd © 1960 Alan Garner; An extract on pp.9-10 from *Linnaeus: Organising Nature* by Liz Miles reprinted by permission of HarperCollins Publishers Ltd © HarperCollins Publishers Ltd 2017; An extract on pp.16-17 from *Hard Times: Growing up in the Victorian Age* reprinted by permission of HarperCollins Publishers Ltd © 2008 Jillian Powell; An extract on pp.18-19 from *Nicholas Nickleby* reprinted by permission of HarperCollins Publishers Ltd © 2015 Julie Berry; An extract on pp.27-29 from *Coral Reefs* by Moira Butterfield reprinted by permission of HarperCollins Publishers Ltd © HarperCollins Publishers Ltd 2016; An extract on pp.35-36 from *Virginia Hall: World War II Spy* reprinted by permission of HarperCollins Publishers Ltd © 2012 Adrian Bradbury; An extract on pp.44-46 from *Daybreak* reprinted by permission of HarperCollins Publishers Ltd © 2012 Ally Kennen; An extract on pp.54-56 from *Ade Adepitan: A Paralympian's Story* by Ade Adepitan reprinted by permission of HarperCollins Publishers Ltd © HarperCollins Publishers Ltd 2013; An extract on pp.57-58 from *Balancing Act* reprinted by permission of HarperCollins Publishers Ltd © 2014 Ali Sparkes.

IMAGES

p.8 Kevin Mallon/Shutterstock; p.9 Illustration by Jim Mitchell (Advocate Art) reprinted by permission of HarperCollins Publishers Ltd © HarperCollins Publishers Ltd 2017; p.16 Chronicle/Alamy Stock Photo; p.19 Illustration by Ismael Pinteño reprinted by permission of HarperCollins Publishers Ltd © HarperCollins Publishers Ltd 2015; p.25 Helenaa/Shutterstock; p.26 Ihnatovich Maryia/Shutterstock; p.27 Lotus_studio/Shutterstock; p.29 Val_Iva/Shutterstock; p.35t Illustration by Lee Sullivan and Piers Sanford reprinted by permission of HarperCollins Publishers Ltd © HarperCollins Publishers Ltd 2012; p.35b Apic/Getty Images; p.37 © HarperCollins Publishers Ltd 2019; p.44 Reprinted by permission of HarperCollins Publishers Ltd © 2012 Liz Monahan; p.45 Reprinted by permission of HarperCollins Publishers Ltd © 2012 Liz Monahan; p.47 © HarperCollins Publishers Ltd 2019; p.54 Andrew Redington/Getty; p.55 © Ade Adepitan; p.56 George S de Blonsky/Alamy Stock Photo; p.57 Illustration by Chris Chalik reprinted by permission of HarperCollins Publishers Ltd © HarperCollins Publishers Ltd 2014; p.58 Illustration by Chris Chalik reprinted by permission of HarperCollins Publishers Ltd © HarperCollins Publishers Ltd 2014.

Contents

How to use this book

Introduction

Collins *Reading Comprehension Progress Tests* have been designed to give you a consistent whole-school approach to teaching and assessing reading comprehension. Each photocopiable book covers the required reading comprehension objectives from the 2014 Primary English National Curriculum. For teachers in Scotland, the books can offer guidance and structure that is not provided in the Curriculum for Excellence Experiences and Outcomes or Benchmarks.

As standalone tests, independent of any teaching and learning scheme, the Collins *Reading Comprehension Progress Tests* provide a structured way to assess progress in reading comprehension skills, to help you identify areas for development, and to provide evidence towards expectations for each year group.

Assessment of higher order reading skills

At the end of Key Stage 1 and Key Stage 2, children are assessed on their ability to demonstrate reading comprehension. This is done through national tests (SATs) accompanied by teacher assessment. Collins *Reading Comprehension Progress Tests* have been designed to provide children with opportunities to explore a range of texts whilst building familiarity with the format, language and style of the SATs. Using the tests with your classes each half-term will offer you a snapshot of your pupils' progress throughout the year.

The tests draw on a wide range of text types, from original stories, poems and playscripts to engaging non-fiction material. The questions follow the style and format of SATs papers and are pitched at a level appropriate to the year group. The tests provide increasing challenge within each year group and across the school. Regular use of the progress tests should help children to develop and practise the necessary skills required to complete the national tests with confidence.

How to use this book

In this book, you will find six photocopiable half-termly tests. Each child will need a copy of the test. You will also find a Curriculum Map on page 6 indicating the aspects of the Content Domain covered in each test across the year group. These have been cross-referenced with the appropriate age-related statements from the National Curriculum.

The Year 6 tests demonstrate standard SATs-style questions and mirror the recognised KS2 format of whole texts followed by an answer booklet. Each test includes two contrasting texts. There is no set amount of time for completion of these tests, but a guide is to allow approximately one minute per mark. However, the length of text increases in Tests 5 and 6 so it is important to develop children's reading stamina and fluency and teach them how to retrieve information quickly, efficiently and accurately.

To help you mark the tests, you will find mark schemes that include the number of marks to be awarded, model answers and a reference to the elements of the Content Domain covered by each question.

Test demand

The tests have been written to ensure smooth progression in children's reading comprehension within the book and across the rest of the books in the series. Each test builds on those before it so that children are guided towards the expectations of the SATs at the end of KS1 and KS2.

Year group	Test	Number of texts per test	Length of text per test	Number of marks per test
6	Autumn 1	2	Up to 1000 words in total	30
6	Autumn 2	2	Up to 1000 words in total	30
6	Spring 1	2	Up to 1000 words in total	30
6	Spring 2	2	Up to 1000 words in total	30
6	Summer 1	2	Up to 1400 words in total	30
6	Summer 2	2	Up to 1400 words in total	30

Performance thresholds

The table below provides guidance for assessing how children perform in the tests. Most children should achieve scores at or above the expected standard, with some children working at greater depth and exceeding expectations for their year group. While the thresholds bands do not represent standardised scores, as in the end of key stage SATs, they will give an indication of how pupils are performing against the expected standards for their year group.

Year group	Test	Working towards	Expected	Greater Depth
6	Autumn 1	15 marks or below	16–23 marks	24–30 marks
6	Autumn 2	15 marks or below	16–23 marks	24–30 marks
6	Spring 1	15 marks or below	16–23 marks	24–30 marks
6	Spring 2	15 marks or below	16–23 marks	24–30 marks
6	Summer 1	15 marks or below	16–23 marks	24–30 marks
6	Summer 2	15 marks or below	16–23 marks	24–30 marks

Tracking progress

A record sheet is provided to help you illustrate to children the areas in which their reading comprehension is strong and where they need to develop. A spreadsheet tracker is also provided via **collins.co.uk/assessment/downloads** which enables you to identify whole-class patterns of attainment. This can be used to inform your next teaching and learning steps.

Editable download

All the files are available online in Word and PDF format. Go to **collins.co.uk/assessment/downloads** to find instructions on how to download. The files are password protected and the password clue is included on the website. You will need to use the clue to locate the password in your book.

You can use these editable files to help you meet the specific needs of your class, whether that be by increasing or decreasing the challenge, by reducing the amount of questions, by providing more space for answers or increasing the size of text for specific children.

Year 6 Curriculum map: Yearly overview

National Curriculum objective (Year 6)	Content domain	Test 1 Fiction	Test 1 Non-fiction	Test 2 Non-fiction	Test 2 Fiction	Test 2 Poetry	Test 3 Non-fiction	Test 3 Non-fiction	Test 4 Non-fiction	Test 4 Play-script	Test 5 Fiction	Test 5 Poetry	Test 6 Non-fiction	Test 6 Fiction
Identify and discuss themes and conventions in and across writing.	2f Identify/explain how information/narrative content is related and contributes to meaning as a whole.	●			●	●					●		●	●
Make comparisons within and across texts.	2h Make comparisons within the text.		●			●							●	●
Discuss the meaning of words in context.	2a Give/explain the meaning of words in context.	●	●	●	●	●	●		●	●		●	●	●
Draw inferences such as inferring characters' feelings, thoughts and motives from their actions, and justifying inferences with evidence.	2d Make inferences from the text / explain and justify inferences with evidence from the text	●	●	●	●	●	●		●	●	●	●	●	●
Predict what might happen from details stated and implied.	2e Predict what might happen from details stated and implied.				●		●							
Summarise the main ideas drawn from more than one paragraph (or verse) identifying key details that support the main ideas.	2c Summarise main ideas from more than one paragraph.	●	●	●	●	●	●		●	●		●	●	●
Identify how language, structure and presentation contribute to meaning.	2g Identify/explain how meaning is enhanced through choice of words and phrases.	●	●		●	●					●	●		
Discuss and evaluate how authors use language, including figurative language, considering the impact on the reader.	2g Identify/explain how meaning is enhanced through choice of words and phrases.	●			●	●				●	●	●		
Distinguish between statements of fact and opinion.	2d Make inferences from the text / explain and justify inferences with evidence from the text.			●				●	●				●	
Retrieve and record information/identify key details from fiction and non-fiction.	2b Retrieve and record information / identify key details from fiction and non-fiction.	●	●	●	●	●			●	●	●	●	●	●
Provide reasoned justification to support views.	2d Make inferences from the text / explain and justify inferences with evidence from the text.	●	●	●	●	●	●		●	●	●	●	●	●

From *The Weirdstone of Brisingamen*

by Alan Garner

The guard knocked on the door of the compartment as he went past.

"Wilmslow fifteen minutes!"

"Thank you!" shouted Colin.

Susan began to clear away the debris of the journey – apple cores, orange peel, food wrappings, magazines – while Colin pulled down their luggage from the rack. And within three minutes they were both poised on the edge of their seats, case in hand and mackintosh over one arm, caught, like every traveller before or since, in that limbo of journey's end, when there is nothing to do and no time to relax. Those last miles were the longest of all.

The platform of Wilmslow station was thick with people, and more spilled off the train, but Colin and Susan had no difficulty in recognising Gowther Mossock among those waiting. As the tide of passengers broke round him and surged through the gates, leaving the children lonely at the far end of the platform, he waved his hand and came striding towards them.

He was an oak of a man: not over tall, but solid as a crag, and barrelled with flesh, bone, and muscles. His face was round and polished; blue eyes crinkled to the humour of his mouth. A tweed jacket strained across his back, and his legs, curved like the timbers of an old house, were clad in breeches, which tucked into thick woollen stockings just above the swelling calves. A felt hat, old and formless, was on his head, and hob-nailed boots struck sparks from the platform as he walked.

"Hallo! I'm thinking you must be Colin and Susan." His voice was gusty and high-pitched, yet mellow, like an autumn gale.

"That's right," said Colin. "And are you Mr Mossock?"

"I am – but we'll have none of your 'Mr Mossock', if you please. Gowther's my name. Now come on, let's be having you. Bess is getting us some supper, and we're not home yet."

He picked up their cases, and they made their way down the steps to the station yard, where there stood a green farm-cart with high red wheels, and between the shafts was a white horse, with shaggy mane and fetlock.

"Eh up, Scamp!" said Gowther as he heaved the cases into the back of the cart. A brindled lurcher, which had been asleep on a rug, stood and eyed the children warily while they climbed to the seat. Gowther took his place between them, and away they drove under the station bridge on the last stage of their travels.

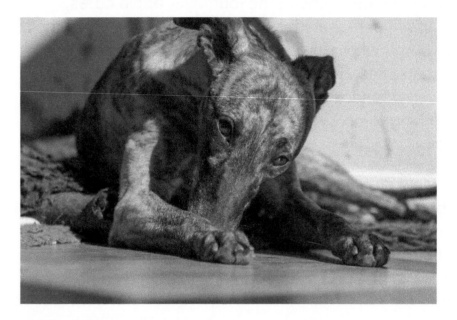

They soon left the village behind and were riding down a tree-bordered lane between fields. They talked of this and that, and the children were gradually accepted by Scamp, who came and thrust his head on to the seat between Susan and Gowther.

Then, "What on earth's *that*?" said Colin.

From *Linnaeus: Organising Nature*

by Liz Miles

Carl Linnaeus was one of the most important and influential scientists who ever lived. He invented a system for naming and classifying living things, which is still in use today, and went on scientific expeditions to remote parts of the world. His adventurous life and his work have inspired scientists ever since.

Expedition to Lapland

In Linnaeus's time, people rarely travelled to the northern parts of Sweden, Norway and Finland, known as Lapland. It was seen as a mysterious wilderness, where people lived very different nomadic lives and spoke an unfamiliar language.

But Linnaeus longed to go to Lapland to find out about the plants that grew in the cold climate, and learn more about the people.

Linnaeus knew that exploring Lapland's wildlife and its people would help his career. But he could only go if he could get a grant from the Royal Society of Uppsala. He put in a request, explaining how important it was to explore the area's rich wildlife and suggesting he might discover valuable minerals that would help make Sweden rich.

On a visit home, he told his parents of his plans. His mother was worried because so few travellers had visited the area before. She hoped Linnaeus wouldn't get the grant. However, his father understood that the trek could be an important step in his son's career.

Linnaeus was thrilled when he got the grant in 1732. He excitedly packed the things he needed for the expedition. At the time, there were no lightweight tents or special clothes for crossing mountains and snow-covered forests.

His transport was a horse.

Linnaeus's list for the expedition:

a coat	sword
second-hand leather breeches	magnifying glass
a wig	spy-glass (telescope)
a cap	a gauze veil (to protect
boots	head from midges)
bag	a journal
shirts	paper
night caps	own works on birds
pen and ink	and plants

Throughout the expedition, Linnaeus gathered specimens of wildlife to take home. He was excited about the plants he discovered, especially the lichens and mosses that are common in Lapland. He wrote notes in his journal and drew pictures to record what he saw.

Linnaeus and the Sami

The Sami people are the native people of Lapland. When Linnaeus spent time with them, he observed them following herds of reindeer, which spend the winter in the lower forests, and the summer in the mountains. The Sami traditionally lived mainly on fish and the meat of reindeer. They used reindeer skins to make their tents and clothes. Linnaeus was eager to see their customs and traditions. Like all explorers, he was curious, but this was also part of the scientific study he'd promised to the Royal Society of Uppsala in return for their grant.

Linnaeus drew pictures of the Sami's customs. For example, he watched how they built their tents. The tents were temporary because the Sami travelled with their reindeer.

Linnaeus noticed how healthy the Sami were. He thought of a number of reasons: pure air and pure water, no overeating, and peaceful minds as there was no squabbling or jealousy. All these things are still thought to be important for a healthy life.

Name: Class: Date:

Questions 1–10 are about **The Weirdstone of Brisingamen**
(pages 7–8).

1   Which **two** statements are correct?

✓ Tick **two**.

Susan and Colin are at the start of a train journey. ☐

There is a station at Wilmslow. ☐

Susan and Colin are at the end of a train journey. ☐

Colin was the guard. ☐

2 marks

2   **Find** and **copy** the word that means 'rubbish', used to describe the mess that Susan clears up in the carriage.

_____

1 mark

3   If the children were *poised on the edge of their seats, case in hand and mackintosh over one arm*, how do you think they might have been feeling?

_____

1 mark

4   According to the text, which miles were *the longest of all*, and why do you think that might be the case?

_____

_____

2 marks

5 Explain the phrase: *more [people] spilled off the train*.

_____

1 mark

6 We are given the impression that Mr Mossock is a strong man. Choose **two** phrases from the text that illustrate this.

1. _____

_____

2. _____

_____

2 marks

7 The author has used the word *barrelled*. How does that help us to picture Mr Mossock?

_____

_____

1 mark

8 Put ticks (✔) in the table to show which of these statements are **true** and which are **false**.

	True	False
Mr Mossock was friendly.		
Mr Mossock was getting them some supper.		
Mr Mossock had a deep voice.		
Mr Mossock liked to be called Gowther.		

2 marks

9 **a)** **Find** and **copy** evidence from the text which shows that the lurcher was not very pleased to see the children at first.

_____

b) Explain why you think this might be.

_____

_____

                                                    _____
                                                    2 marks

10 Do you think this story is set in modern times? Circle **Yes** or **No**, and then, using the whole the text, give **two** reasons to support your answer.

            Yes   **No**

1. _____

_____

2. _____

_____

                                                    _____
                                                    2 marks

> Questions 11–20 are about *Linnaeus: Organising Nature* (pages 9–10).

11 The first paragraph introduces the scientist, Carl Linnaeus.

Find and **copy three** adjectives the author has used to describe him.

_____ _____ _____

                                                    _____
                                                    1 mark

12 Which word means the same as *expedition*?

✓ Tick **one**.

experiment ☐

holiday ☐

journey ☐

exhibition ☐

1 mark

13 According to the text, where is Lapland?

_____

1 mark

14 Why do you think Linnaeus suggested to the Royal Society of Uppsala that he might find *valuable minerals that would help make Sweden rich*?

_____

_____

1 mark

15 Linnaeus's parents had contrasting views about his expedition. What were they?

_____

_____

_____

2 marks

16 In what year did Linnaeus get the grant he needed?

_____

1 mark

17 Put ticks (✔) in the table to show which of these items might be taken on an expedition in 1732 and which items might be taken today. Some may appear in both columns.

	1732	Today
a coat		
second-hand leather breeches		
a mobile phone		
a lightweight tent		
a bag		
a sword		

2 marks

18 Linnaeus drew pictures of the plants. Why do you think he didn't take photographs?

_____

1 mark

19 Linnaeus also recorded information about the Sami.

Using the text, give **two** examples of things he learned.

1. _____

2. _____

2 marks

20 What impression do you get of Linnaeus? Support your answer with evidence from the **whole** text.

_____

_____

_____

2 marks

From *Hard Times: Growing up in the Victorian Age*

by Jillian Powell

Glossary	
abacus	a simple counting device using beads on rows
governess	a woman teacher employed in a private household
Industrial Revolution	the rapid growth of industry in Britain from the late 1700s throughout the 1800s because of inventions including steam-powered machinery
mass-produced	made in large numbers by machines
pinafore	a dress with a sleeveless top, worn over a blouse

Children in Victorian times lived very different lives from yours today.

Queen Victoria ruled Britain from 1837 to 1901. Many of the grand buildings in Britain, such as shops and banks, bridges and railway stations, were built in Victorian times. Photography was one of the Victorians' many inventions, along with the railways.

Britain was a rich and powerful nation under Queen Victoria. The **Industrial Revolution** was changing people's lives as well as their cities and towns. Mills, mines and factories were making **mass-produced** goods for the first time, and the railways meant that goods as well as people could travel faster than before.

In early Victorian times, most children did not go to school. There were no free state schools as there are today. There were only church or charity schools, or dame schools run by old women in their homes. Rich children usually had a tutor or **governess** to teach them at home, and boys sometimes went on to a private day or boarding school.

Some poor children were sent to ragged schools, which gave them food and lodgings as well as lessons, but many had no schooling as they had to work to bring in money for the family. After 1870, local School Boards were set up to open a school in every town and village.

The bright classroom displays, computers and libraries in your schools are very different from the bare, stark classrooms of Victorian schools. They were dimly lit by gaslights, and the only heating was a smoky stove in the corner. It was sometimes so cold in winter that the inkwells in the desks froze over. Boys and girls often went in by separate doors and sat in rows of wooden desks all facing the teacher at the front. Most girls wore **pinafores** over their dresses and boys wore caps, trousers and jackets.

The only other classroom equipment was some books, an **abacus** for mathematics and a globe for geography. On the walls there might have been a picture of Queen Victoria. Children spent most of the day copying from the blackboard. The main subjects were reading, writing, arithmetic and religious instruction. Children wrote in chalk on slate boards that they could wipe clean and use again. The teacher used a whistle and a cane to keep strict discipline, punishing pupils by caning them or making them stand in the corner for hours wearing a pointed dunce's cap.

Key dates for children

1833	The Factory Act bans children under 9 from working in textile mills.
1842	The Coal Mines Act bans females of all ages and boys under 10 from working underground.
1844	The Ragged Schools Union is formed.
1844	The Factory Act limits working hours for children aged between 9 and 13 to six hours a day.
1870	Dr Thomas Barnardo sets up his first home for orphans.
1870	The Education Act gives powers to Schools Boards to start up schools.
1873	Children under 8 years old are banned from working on farms.
1875	The practice of using climbing boys is banned.
1880	The Education Act makes it compulsory for children aged between 5 and 10 to attend school.
1891	The government makes education free and compulsory for all children.

From *Nicholas Nickleby*

by Charles Dickens (retold by Julie Berry)

He woke in the morning to Mrs Squeers' voice.

"Where's the school spoon?" she cried. "If that Smike's gone and lost it, he'll sleep in the barn for a month."

"A school *spoon*?" asked Nicholas.

"It's brimstone morning," snapped Mrs Squeers.

Mr Squeers explained. "We feed the boys brimstone – that's sulphur – and treacle one day a month to purify their blood. Keeps 'em from getting ill."

"He might as well know the truth, Squeery."

Mrs Squeers rummaged through every cupboard.

"We don't care a fig for their blood. Sulphur and treacle cost much less than breakfast and dinner. Good for them, good for us. But I need my spoon to dose them, for those nasty, disobedient boys won't swallow it like they should."

Nicholas was horrified. "Who's Smike?"

"A wretched, stupid creature," said Squeers cheerfully. "He was a student, till his people stopped paying. Nobody claimed him. We keep him out of kindness and make him work for us."

Nicholas rose, dressed, and followed Mr Squeers into the schoolroom. What he saw made his heart sink.

The dark dirty schoolroom lacked most of its windowpanes. Paper patches were all that blocked the cold. What few school books Nicholas saw were old, torn and stained.

But the room was nothing compared to the students themselves. They were the scrawniest, palest, sickliest children Nicholas had ever seen. They coughed. They stooped. They had vacant looks in their eyes.

Mrs Squeers entered the room with her brimstone and treacle. She pinched each boy's nose. Tipped his head back, and shoved her spoon down his throat, heaped with her sticky, foul-smelling brew.

Any boy who vomited the disgusting mixture back up was forced to swallow another large dose.

This was only the beginning of Dotheboys Hall.

Mr Squeers had no business calling himself a schoolmaster. He could barely read or write. He gathered the pupils for pointless lessons lasting only a few minutes, then sent them out in the cold to shovel snow, rake stables and do other chores.

"That's what we call a practical education, Nickleby," boasted Squeers. "They learn more from experience than from books."

Nicholas wondered why they wanted an assistant teacher at Dotheboys Hall, if no learning ever happened there.

Name:	Class:	Date:

> Questions 1–10 are about *Hard Times: Growing up in the Victorian Age* (pages 16–17).

1 When did Queen Victoria's reign end?

_____

1 mark

2 **Find** and **copy one** word that describes the buildings from the Victorian age.

_____

1 mark

3 **Copy** the definition given in the text for the word *mass-produced*.

_____

1 mark

4 Put ticks (✓) in the table to show which of these statements are **true** and which are **false**.

In Victorian times:	True	False
most rich children had a governess or tutor.		
most children went to school.		
there were no boarding schools.		
some poor children had to go out to work.		

1 mark

5 *ragged schools, which gave them food and lodgings*

Explain the word *lodgings*.

_____

1 mark

6 Draw **four** lines to match each date to an event.

1842	Education was made free and compulsory for all children.
1870	Attending school became compulsory for children aged between 5 and 10.
1880	Boys under 10 and all females were banned from working down the mines.
1891	School Boards were allowed to set up new schools.

1 mark

7 *makes education free and compulsory for all children*

Explain the word *compulsory*.

_____

1 mark

8 What clothing was worn by children in Victorian schools?

_____

_____

_____

2 marks

9 Put ticks (✓) in the table to show which of these are **fact** and which are **opinion**.

	Fact	Opinion
Victorian children sat in rows.		
Modern classrooms have bright displays.		
Classrooms were lit by gaslights.		
Canes were used to punish pupils.		

2 marks

10 Would you like to have grown up in Victorian times?

Circle **Yes** or **No** and give **three reasons**, using the text to support your answer.

Yes   No

1. _____

_____

2. _____

_____

3. _____

_____

3 marks

Questions 11–20 are about **Nicholas Nickleby** (pages 18–19).

11 How long would Smike have to sleep in the barn if he took the *school spoon*?

_____

1 mark

12 Why did Mrs Squeers need the *school spoon*?

_____

1 mark

13 *Mrs Squeers rummaged through every cupboard.*

Explain the word *rummaged.*

_____

1 mark

14 Why did Mrs Squeers really give the boys brimstone and treacle?
Support your answer with evidence from the text.

_____

_____

_____

2 marks

15 *Nobody claimed him. We keep him out of kindness and make him work for us.*

What does the word *claimed* mean here and what can we learn from these two sentences?

_____

_____

_____

2 marks

16 Explain the phrase *made his heart sink.*

_____

1 mark

17 What do you think it was like in the Dotheboys Hall classroom? Use evidence from the text to support your answer.

_____

_____

_____

2 marks

18 What is your impression of Mr and Mrs Squeers? Support your answer with evidence from the text.

_____

_____

_____

_____

_____

3 marks

19 List **two** facts you have learned about brimstone and treacle.

1. _____

2. _____

2 marks

20 Do you predict that Nicholas will be happy in his new job as assistant teacher in Dotheboys Hall?

Justify your answer with evidence from the text.

_____

_____

_____

1 mark

All Things Beautiful – *An Anthology of Poems*

by Stephanie Austwick

(Try to guess what each poem is describing as you read it. Clue: they are all found in a garden.)

1. A burst of colour,
   A flash,
   A glint,
   A fleeting shadow,
   A glimmer, a shimmer,
   A flit and a flutter,
   A glancing, dancing ballerina
   Pirouetting on the perfumed breeze.

2. Hurrying,
   Scurrying,
   Men on a mission,
   Things to do,
   Places to be,
   We're late, we're late
   For an important date.
   In and out
   And up and down
   And out and in
   And down and up.
   Marching onwards.
   Like a miniature army
   Of tiny black dots.
   Who's following who?

3. Slipping and sliding and gliding lazily between the dense, overgrown maze.
   Silently ploughing an underground furrow through the sticky red earth.
   Gracefully tracing a pathway in the moist darkness.
   Snake-like.
   Slinking slowly over sprawling roots.
   Unheard. Unseen. Unnoticed.
   Except by blackbirds and small boys.

4. There's a predator in our garden,
    He arrived at dead of night.
    I see him from my window.
    He gives me quite a fright.
    His beady eyes, his ruby coat,
    His white-tipped tail
    Which seems to float.

    He stops, he sniffs,
    He stalks around,
    His padded paws
    Create no sound,
    Until…
    He clatters and crashes,
    Creates such a din.
    My nightly visitor
    Has found the bin!

5. Squishy and slimy,
    Sliding through the rain,

    Greasy and grimy,
    On the move again.

    Leaching and leaking,
    Snoozing and oozing,
    Seeping and weeping,
    You leave a trail behind.

    You have no friends,
    But you don't seem to mind.

6. Perfume fills the air,
    A heady hint of summer
    Petals of fine silk.

From *Coral Reefs*

by Moira Butterfield

Amazing ecosystems

A coral reef is a big underwater structure made of a stony substance called limestone.

It's made by millions of tiny creatures called stony or hard corals.

Living corals, marine plants and animals all live on top of the reef structure.

A coral reef is an ecosystem where there's lots of natural life. Although coral reefs cover less than 1% of the ocean floor, they're home to around 25% of the world's marine animals and plants.

Where to find reefs

Coral reefs grow mainly in shallow warm water, so most of them are found in the warm oceans of the tropics, the area of the world on either side of the equator.

Conditions have to be just right for corals to grow. Most of them need plenty of sunlight, which is why the seawater around them must be shallow and clear. It must be roughly the temperature of a lukewarm bath, with just the right amount of saltiness.

A few rare corals grow in deep cold water.

Record-breaking reefs

The biggest reef on the planet is the Great Barrier Reef off the northeast coast of Australia. It's the world's largest structure made by living creatures.

The world's longest reefs

1. Great Barrier Reef
   Length: 2,300 kilometres
   Location: in the Coral Sea near Australia

2. Red Coral Reef
   Length 1,900 kilometres
   Location: in the Red Sea near Israel, Egypt and Djibouti

3. New Caledonian Barrier Reef
   Length: 1,500 kilometres
   Location: in the Pacific Ocean, near the island of New Caledonia

How old are reefs?

Most of today's coral reefs have taken between 5,000 and 10,000 years to grow.

Round boulder-shaped corals only grow by around five to 25 millimetres a year. Smaller branched corals can grow by as much as 20 centimetres a year.

The oldest living coral ever found was a species called black coral, growing off the coast of Hawaii. Tests showed it to be 4,265 years old. It grew between four and 35 micrometres a year (a human hair measure around 80 micrometres across).

How is a reef built?

Tiny baby corals called planula float in the ocean. They settle on underwater rocks near land and grow into soft mini coral bodies called polyps. The polyps of the stony coral family protect themselves by making a hard limestone cup-shaped skeleton around their base. They produce the limestone in their bodies using material they absorb from the sea around them.

When a polyp dies, it leaves its little stone skeleton behind and new corals grow on top. Eventually, enough polyps grow and die off for the limestone to build up into a reef.

All about polyps

A stony coral polyp has a body that looks like a little bag. There's an opening for a mouth, with tentacles around it. Coral polyps are usually nocturnal, which means they hide in their skeletons during the day and extend their tentacles out to feed at night.

Stony corals are very small – only around one to three millimetres wide. They live together in colonies. Imagine how many billions of polyps it took to build the Great Barrier Reef!

Human danger

Pollution kills coral. Chemicals and sewage that run into the sea can kill coral. Fertilisers washed from farmland can make algae grow more strongly, choking the reef.

Soil particles called sediment can run into seawater when forests are cut down onshore, cleared for wood or for new building land. The particles can block out sunlight, helping to kill the coral.

Rubbish tipped into the ocean can kill coral reef creatures. Sea turtles can mistake plastic bags for jellyfish and eat them, blocking their stomachs so they starve to death. Lost fishing nets can tangle up on reefs and trap creatures too.

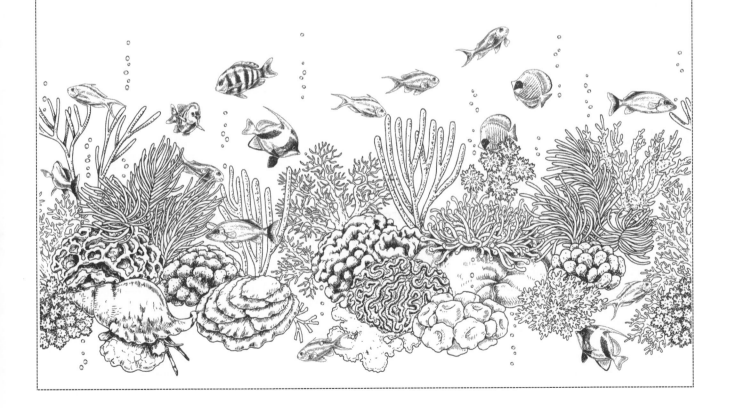

Name:	Class:	Date:

> Questions 1–10 are about **All Things Beautiful – An Anthology of Poems** (pages 25–26).

1 What is an *anthology* of poems?

_____

1 mark

Read **Poem 1**.

2 Which insect do you think this poem is describing?

Insect: _____

Using the text, give **two** reasons to justify your answer.

1. _____

2. _____

2 marks

3 *A fleeting shadow*

Explain the word *fleeting*:

_____

1 mark

Read **Poem 2**.

4 This poem is about an army of ants.

Apart from being small, what impression do you get of the ants from this poem? Support your answer with evidence from the text.

_____

_____

_____

2 marks

Read **Poem 3**.

5 The movement of the worm in this poem contrasts with the movement of the ants in **Poem 2**.

Compare the two poems and explain how you feel the poet has created this contrast.

Support your answer with reference to **both** poems.

_____

_____

_____

_____

2 marks

Read **Poem 4**.

6 What creature do you think the nightly predator might be?

Give evidence from the text to support your answer.

_____

1 mark

7 *His white-tipped tail,*
Which seems to float.

Why do you think the white tip of his tail might look as if it's floating?

_____

_____

1 mark

Read **Poem 5**.

8 How do you think the poet feels about the slug in this poem? Support your answer with reference to the text.

_____

_____

_____

2 marks

Read **Poem 6**.

9 This is a haiku about a rose. Why do you think the poet has used the metaphor _petals of fine silk_?

_____

1 mark

After reading the **whole anthology**:

10 Consider all five poems. Which one do you like best and why?

Support your answers with reference to the text.

_____

_____

_____

2 marks

Questions 11–20 are about **_Coral Reefs_** (pages 27–29).

11 According to the text, what is a coral reef?

_____

_____

1 mark

12 Put ticks (✔) in the table to show which of these statements are **true** and which are **false**.

	True	False
All coral reefs like cold water.		
Most reefs are found in the tropics.		
Sunlight is important for coral reefs to grow.		
Water needs to be deep.		

2 marks

13 Circle **two** words that mean the same as *rare*.

unusual   different   uncommon   popular

1 mark

14 Read the sections **Record-breaking reefs** and **The world's longest reefs**.

Explain, **exactly**, where the Great Barrier Reef is located.

1. _____

2. _____

2 marks

15 Draw **four** lines to match the fact to the reef.

Red Coral Reef	Length: 1,500 kilometres
New Caledonian Barrier Reef	Biggest reef on the planet
Great Barrier Reef	Location: near Israel, Egypt and Djibouti

1 mark

16 How old is the oldest living coral ever found?

_____

1 mark

17 Number the sentences below from **1** to **4** to show the order in which they happen.

The polyps die and leave a little stone skeleton behind. ☐

Tiny baby corals float in the ocean. ☐

Enough polyps grow and die to build up into a reef. ☐

The polyps protect themselves with hard limestone. ☐

1 mark

18 Record **two** facts you have learned about stony coral polyps.

1. _____

2. _____

2 marks

19 According to the text, what is the meaning of the word *sediment*?

_____

1 mark

20 **Pollution is destroying our oceans.**

Do you agree with this statement?

Justify your answer with reference to the text.

_____

_____

_____

_____

3 marks

From *Virginia Hall: World War II Spy*

by Adrian Bradbury

Spies

When countries go to war against each other, spies play an important role. A key element of war is knowing your enemy's strengths and weaknesses. The more information you have, the better you can plan. The spy's task is to gather this information without the enemy knowing and pass it back to his or her commanders.

Any information might turn out to be useful. How many people does the enemy have? What battle plans do they have? Who are their leaders? How can we get to them? And, of course, how are *they* spying on *us*?

Some spies operate in their own country. They betray their homeland for a variety of reasons: money, fame or dissatisfaction with their government, for instance.

Others may be blackmailed by an enemy into spying on their own country, and forced into revealing its secrets.

Some spies are sent into enemy countries to find out what's happening and report back. They might build up a network of contacts in that country to help them. Their life is full of danger. They live in fear of exposure, day and night. These people are known as secret agents.

Virginia Hall was one of the bravest and the best.

Endgame

There is little doubt that Virginia Hall, and many spies like her, played a huge part in the Allies' ultimate victory in World War II. Without their daring deeds, British and American generals would not have had the top-secret information needed to form their battle plans.

The spies' bravery not only saved soldiers' lives, but helped to shorten the war, preventing further hardships and suffering for millions of civilians. Their lives were spent in constant fear, waiting every minute for a knock at the door, or expecting someone to stop them as they walked on the street.

The risks for a spy were great – almost certain death if they were captured. The rewards for a spy were few. Spies might spend the rest of their lives without realising the role they had played in saving their country from disaster.

Spying in the 21st century

As the race to develop nuclear weapons gathered pace in the 1950s and 1960s, the role of the spy became even more vital. These agents operated in the backstreets and offices of Moscow, Berlin, London and other major capitals. Each government fought to keep its own secrets safe while stealing those of its rivals.

Today, almost every country in the world has its own intelligence service, but most information is now gathered from computers and mobile phones.

Sophisticated listening stations pick up phone conversations from all over the world; computers are hacked, and texts and emails are monitored. Satellites and CCTV cameras watch from the skies and on the ground.

However, despite the use of modern technology, spies still operate in much the same way as Virginia Hall did during World War II. Experts suggest that there are now more spies than ever operating in our cities, gathering information as they wait and watch.

From the screenplay *The End of the Line*

by Stephanie Austwick

Two friends stumble across a disused factory.

An exciting adventure or a deadly discovery?

Scene 3: The next morning.

Jed and Ali are sitting on a wall, overlooking the waste ground. They are both deep in thought. Eventually, Jed breaks the silence.

Jed: I'm not going back.

Ali: Why?

Jed: *(aggressively)* I don't want to. Why do you have to keep going on about it? I just don't want to go back there, and that's that. You're like a track on repeat. Give it a rest!

Ali: All I said was …

Jed: *(exasperated)* You're doing it again. I AM **NOT** GOING BACK TO BANROCK! How many more times?

    There is another awkward silence. Ali fixes his eyes on Jed but Jed refuses to meet his gaze.

Ali: *(realisation dawning)* You're scared. You don't want to go back because you're scared. You pretend you're all brave and stuff and really …

Jed: *(jumping down off the wall and turning to face Ali)* I AM NOT SCARED! Stop going on about it! It's just a factory. A boring, empty old factory. There's nothing there. I don't get why you want to go back there. I don't see the attraction, OK? *(Jed turns sharply and starts to walk away. Ali follows.)*

Ali: Yeah, but when you ran down those stairs you were as white as a sheet. And you didn't stop running 'til we got back to your place. You must have seen something. What I don't get is why you aren't saying anything. What did you see? Jed? *(Jed increases his pace.)* Jed? Wait!

Jed: *(turning)* Nothing, OK? I didn't see anything. Now, get lost!

(Jed runs off – Ali doesn't follow.)

Shaz: *(appearing round the corner)* Hi Ali. Where's the Jedi master going?

Ali: Dunno.

Shaz: *(teasing)* You two had a fight or something?

Ali: Yeah … sort of. He's just being really weird.

Shaz: *(laughing)* Oh what's new! He'll be back in …

Ali: No. *Really* weird. We went to Banrock last night – you know, the old factory? – just for something to do. We found a door that was unlocked so we went in for a snoop around and it was really cool. There were loads of old machines, and material, and lots of dummies – you know, the sort they have in shop windows …

Shaz: Mannequins.

Ali: What?

Shaz: They're called mannequins.

Ali: Whatever. Anyway, we were messing around with them – putting their arms in different positions and pretending they were talking and stuff – and we were having a right laugh. Then Jed went up these metal stairs, to an office or something, which had windows overlooking the factory, but the blinds were all closed. I stayed downstairs. Then suddenly, he came crashing down the stairs, three at a time, and legged it. Now he won't say a word.

Shaz: What was up there?

Ali: That's what I mean – he won't say. I wanted to go back for another look round, maybe get one of those … *manny-things* as a mascot for the club, but he absolutely refuses. It's really odd!

Shaz: Perhaps he saw a ghost?

(Ali shoots Shaz a withering look.)

Shaz: *(defensively)* Well he must have seen something!

Ali: Yes … but a ghost? *Seriously*?

Shaz: Well why didn't you go up and have a look yourself?

Ali: I … I … was following Jed. I didn't know what was going on.

Shaz: *(thinks for a moment)* I'll come!

Ali: What?

Shaz: I'll come with you! Back to the factory.

Ali: *(hands up; mock-shocked)* But you're … a *girl*!

Shaz: *(giving Ali a playful push)* DO **NOT** even go there!

Name:	Class:	Date:

> **Questions 1–9 are about *Virginia Hall: World War II Spy*
> (pages 35–36).**

Read the section **Spies**.

1   Using the text, complete this sentence:

The more information you have …

✓ Tick **one**.

the easier it is to be a spy. ☐

the better you can plan. ☐

the more times you can operate in your own country. ☐

the more often you can go into enemy countries. ☐

1 mark

2   **Find** and **copy one** word that means 'someone working for the other side'.

_____

1 mark

3   Identify **two** types of information that might be obtained by a spy during wartime.

1.   _____

_____

2.   _____

_____

2 marks

4 Put ticks (✔) in the table to show which of these statements are **fact** and which are **opinion**.

	Fact	Opinion
Spies passed on top-secret information.		
Virginia Hall was a spy.		
Virginia Hall was one of the bravest spies.		

1 mark

5 What impression do you have of World War II spies? Support your answer using evidence from the text.

_____

_____

_____

2 marks

Read the section **Spying in the 21st century**.

6 *the role of the spy became even more vital*

Give an alternative word that could be used instead of *vital* in this sentence.

_____

1 mark

7 According to the text, what other term is used instead of spies?

_____

1 mark

8   How has spying changed in the 21st century? Give **two** examples from the text.

1. _____

_____

2. _____

_____

2 marks

9   After reading this text, would you like to be a spy?

Give **two** reasons for your answer, using information gathered from the **whole** text.

_____

_____

_____

2 marks

Questions 10–20 are about *The End of the Line* (pages 37–38).

10   Why do you think did Jed says, *You're like a track on repeat?*

_____

1 mark

11   **Find** and **copy** the stage direction which demonstrates that Jed was getting annoyed with Ali's constant questioning.

_____

1 mark

12 When had the two boys been to the old factory?

_____

1 mark

13 How do you think Ali might be feeling after the visit to the old factory?

Give **two** alternative answers with references to the text.

1. _____

_____

2. _____

_____

2 marks

14 Put ticks (✔) in the table to show which of these are **true** and which are **false**.

	True	False
Ali accused Jed of being scared.		
Jed wanted to go back to the factory.		
Jed admitted he was scared.		
Jed was white when he ran down the stairs.		

2 marks

15 Explain the following words:

a) _snoop_ _____

b) _mannequin_ _____

2 marks

16 How do you think Shaz feels about Ali and Jed falling out? Give evidence from the text to support your answer.

_____

_____

_____

2 marks

17 What do you think was produced at Banrock Factory?

_____

1 mark

18 What is meant by a _withering look_ and why do you think Ali looked at Shaz in this way?

_____

_____

_____

2 marks

19 Number the sentences below from **1** to **4** to show the order in which they happened.

They were playing with the mannequins.

They found an unlocked door.

Jed was white as a sheet.

Jed went up the metal stairs.

1 mark

20 How do you think Shaz felt when Ali said she was _a girl_?

Support you answer with evidence from the text.

_____

_____

2 marks

From *Daybreak*

by Ally Kennen

I'm not giving in without a fight. Tomorrow's my birthday and I'm going to be 12 years old. Surely that gives me rights?

"We're not going to make it to the river. I'm so sorry," repeats Mum, her fingers worrying at a loose button on her cardigan.

"But we'll miss it," I yell. I can foresee a great deal more yelling and howling in the next 24 hours.

"There'll be other times, Linnie," says Dad, pulling on his muddy boots.

"There'll never be another five-star bore on my birthday," I fume.

Bores are the wrong name for them. There's nothing boring about a huge tidal wave of water piling down the estuary, high as a house, and dotted with crazy surfers, all mad keen to ride the wave until it swallows them up in its foaming jaws.

Dad reaches over and rubs my head with his scratchy, calloused hands.

"The vet can only come tomorrow morning," he says. "Please try to understand."

I understand all right. Our cows have to be tested for a disease called tuberculosis. And my birthday plans have been cancelled. I shake Dad off, and he and Mum swap their special, extra-weary 'isn't-Linnie-a-pest' look. This look occurs, on average, about four times a day.

"Why can't we move the cows tonight?" I moan. "Then there might be time tomorrow and …"

"It's not safe. It's too dark," says Dad. "We'll move them first thing in the morning."

I'm too angry to sleep.

I'm lying in my bed, and my thoughts are spinning round my head like a washing machine.

I first saw the tidal bore last Spring.

It was registered as a two-star event, which is small compared with tomorrow's five-star bore. Even so, last year was brilliant. We'd walked up the river to a place where the bank sloped gently down. Out of nowhere, the water piled down the river in a steep wave, making the ground shake and shudder under my feet. Dad had to grab my arm and yank me back. If I hadn't moved, I would've been swept away. The water broke off overhanging branches, and clumps of bank just collapsed into the water. Mum went pale – I don't think she expected the bore to be quite so fast and big. We all got soaked in the spray as the wave roared past. I've never seen anything so powerful and exciting as that wave.

Tomorrow's bore will be the biggest of the year; mightier than any I've seen before. Helicopters will be hovering and TV cameras will be filming. In the river, there'll be surfers, people in canoes and even swimmers. Crowds of people will line the banks, and there'll be ice-cream vans, hot-dog stands and balloon-sellers. People will be taking photographs and selling souvenirs.

And the fantastic thing is that this five-star, totally amazing phenomenon is happening on my birthday. This makes it even more magical, like nature has programmed it just for me.

Moon rays give you magical powers. It's the big old moon that will be responsible for tomorrow's five-star bore.

There'll be a spring tide tomorrow, at 9:30 a.m. It's like fate. There's been a big wind and the waves will be huge. It'll feel like a festival on the river banks, with people coming from miles around, stepping out of their lives for a few hours to watch something incredible.

But not me.

I shut my eyes and imagine myself turning off a switch in my head.

The downstairs clock chimes. It's five in the morning. I've been asleep, but now I'm wide awake. I realise I'm no longer 11 years old.

Goodbye 11. It's a little bit sad, but also exciting.

I get out of bed and look out of the window at the farmyard. It's still dark out there, but it won't be for long. The big barn stands empty, the metal roof creaking in the wind. I'm going out.

———————————

Then I have a thought. Just suppose, when Mum and Dad get up this morning, they find the cows are already waiting in the yard. That'd leave us time to see the bore. It's only 16 kilometres to the river. It could be done. A prickle of excitement runs down my back. We'd be back before Anthony, the vet, arrived.

It's about two-and-a-half kilometres down the lane to the farm gate. And there wouldn't be any traffic about at this hour. The lane stretches silver grey behind me. Very soon it'll be dawn. Just suppose …

———————————

But then things start to happen very fast. One minute the cows are all lumped in the far corner of the field, chewing the cud, sleeping or quietly grazing, the next, there's a thunder of hooves. A dark river of cows flows down the hill towards me …

I feel a bolt of alarm. Maybe this wasn't such a good idea, after all.

I start to close the gate, but it's too late. The cows have got the wind behind them and their big, heavy bodies push back the gate, pressing me into the hedge and making it impossible to shut it.

———————————

The cows are stampeding up the road, bucking and trotting and kicking out their legs. The air is full of flies and noise and droplets of mud.

I see Angel at the front of the pack, running up the hill. I clamp my hand over my mouth. The cows are going in the wrong direction.

They mustn't go up the hill as it leads to a crossroads. Here, one road leads to our neighbour's farm. The other road goes down to the meadows and the third way, straight on, is a small lane which, after a kilometre or so, leads steeply down into the very centre of town.

Lost: One Nerve

by Stephanie Austwick

I lost my nerve the other day.
Maybe I dropped it on the way?
Like homework, a key, or a mobile phone –
I'm sure I had it before I left home.

Big Danno was lurking next to the gate.
Stone eyes glinting – full of hate.
"Gimme your money, before it's too late!"

    I was gonna say No!
    I was gonna walk by
    With my nose in the air,
    But I started to cry.
    I'd lost my nerve you see.

Miss Jones was guarding the classroom door.
The line snaked forward – my eyes found the floor.
"Just remember to smile – you'll be great, Class 4."

    I was gonna speak up,
    I was gonna slow down
    And read with expression,
    But I felt myself drown.
    I'd lost my nerve you see.

Mr Pitt was looming, claiming the light,
Eyes like daggers, clipboard held tight
"Don't look so scared, lad – it's not going to bite"

I was gonna climb up
To the very top board,
But my legs turned to jelly,
My anxieties roared.
I'd lost my nerve you see.

Dad was laying the table for tea,
His eyes full of love – but unable to see.
"Did you have a good day, son?" he said to me.

I was gonna say No!
That I'm scared and I'm sad,
That I needed to talk,
But he might think I'm mad.

So I just nodded.

I lost my nerve the other day,
So I'm sending out a plea:
I really need someone out there
To get it back for me.

I lost my nerve the other day.
Haven't seen it for a while.
You'll know it if you find it,
It's wrapped up in my smile.

Name: Class: Date:

Questions 1–12 are about **Daybreak** (pages 44–46).

1 How old will Linnie be on her next birthday?

_____

1 mark

2 How do you think Linnie's mother was feeling when she had to break the news to Linnie that they would not be going to the river? Support your answer with evidence from the text.

_____

_____

_____

2 marks

3 **Find** and **copy two** words from the text that show that Linnie was really angry during this conversation with her parents.

_____   _____

2 marks

4 According to the text, what is a bore and why did Linnie feel that it was the wrong name?

_____

_____

_____

2 marks

5 Why can't Linnie and her family go to the river as planned?

_____

1 mark

6 Explain the difference between the bore Linnie saw last spring and the one she is hoping to go to on her birthday.

_____

_____

_____

2 marks

7 Number the sentences below from **1** to **4** to show the order of events last spring.

Dad grabbed Linnie's arm. ☐

A steep wave of water travelled down the river. ☐

Everyone got soaked. ☐

The family walked to a place on the river bank. ☐

1 mark

8 Apart from it being a five-star bore and it being on her birthday, give **two** other reasons why Linnie might be looking forward to the next day's event.

1. _____

2. _____

2 marks

9 *Just suppose …*

Summarise the plan that was forming in Linnie's mind.

_____

_____

_____

2 marks

10 According to the text, where were the cows *before* Linnie opened the gate?

_____

1 mark

11 Why do you think the author has used the metaphor of a *dark river* to describe the cows in the field?

_____

_____

1 mark

12 How do you think Linnie was feeling at different points in the story? Choose **six different** adjectives to describe her feelings.

How do you think Linnie was feeling when:	Linnie felt …
her mother said they weren't going to the river?	
she went to bed?	
she saw the bore last spring?	
she thinks of her new plan?	
the cows begin to run towards the gate?	
the herd is stampeding down the lane towards the town?	

3 marks

Questions 13–20 are about '**Lost: One Nerve**' (pages 47–48).

13 Explain what is meant by the saying 'to lose your nerve'.

_____

1 mark

14 *I was gonna say No!*
I was gonna walk by
With my nose in the air
But I started to cry …

What do these lines tell us about the boy in the poem?

_____

_____

1 mark

15 What do you think might have been happening in the 'Miss Jones' verse?

_____

1 mark

16 Explain what it meant by Mr Pitt *claiming the light*?

_____

_____

1 mark

17 **Find** and **copy** the word in the text that means the same as *worries*.

_____

1 mark

18 What did the boy do when his Dad asked him if he'd had a good day? Why do you think he did that?

_____

_____

2 marks

19 What can you infer from the fact that the boy says his nerve is wrapped up in his smile?

_____

_____

1 mark

20 **a)** Based on the **whole** poem, choose **three** words to summarise how the boy was feeling that day.

_____ _____ _____

b) Suggest **one** piece of advice you might give him, with reference to a specific incident in the text.

_____

_____

_____

_____

2 marks

Ade Adepitan: A Paralympian's Story

by Ade Adepitan

I came to the UK from Nigeria when I was 3 years old. I'd contracted polio as a child of 15 months and my parents thought I would get better medical treatment in the UK.

My most distinctive memory of Nigeria is a recurring dream I used to have about these

amazing green, lush trees. When I went back to Nigeria in 2007, I saw the trees when we were driving from the airport to my parents' home town and all the memories came flooding back to me.

Both of my parents are from Nigeria. They were teachers with good careers, but there was no treatment for polio. I couldn't walk, and they didn't know if I was going to get worse. My dad felt like he didn't have much choice, so we said goodbye to all our friends and family and moved to east London.

Polio is a waterborne disease – you get it from polluted water and it affects a certain area of your spinal cord, which stops you from sending messages and growing muscles in certain parts of your body. I've got feeling in my legs but no movement. My left side is worse, but the degree of severity increases down my body. For example, it only affects my left hand a little bit – I can move it, but can't hold a pen with it.

When I came to the UK, I was given a caliper splint to wear on my left leg. This consisted of iron rods strapped to my leg which went into a big hospital medical boot – it definitely didn't look cool! Everyone else was wearing trainers and I was wearing these ugly brown boots. Plus, it was really uncomfortable, as the caliper didn't bend, so my left leg was dead straight when I sat down.

I could walk, but in a kind of robotic way. However, using a wheelchair was never really an option. If you could walk at all, it didn't matter what you looked like, or how bad the pain was, walking was always encouraged. My parents really wanted me to walk and had a deep belief that with the support of the caliper and enough practice, I'd get better and would eventually walk on my own.

Schools in the UK at that time were separated into mainstream schools and disability schools. If you were disabled, you went to a school for kids with disabilities – no matter what your disability was or how old you were. If you were able-bodied, you went to a mainstream school.

My dad's intentions were for me to go to a mainstream school. He was so determined that eventually, after about a year of campaigning, one school finally accepted me. I was the first disabled kid in my area to go to a mainstream school and my parents saw it as a real achievement – a step in the right direction towards me having a normal life.

But on my first day, I felt anything but normal!

My mum, who's very flamboyant, had bought me a pair of pink checked flared trousers to wear and combed my hair into a big afro, with a huge side parting. When I arrived, I saw a group of kids playing football in the playground, but they wouldn't let me join in. I guess I was just too different – not only was I one of the few black kids in the school, but I was also disabled. I walked differently, I still had a bit of a Nigerian accent and my name was strange.

However, during the final playtime they stuck me in goal and after the first couple of minutes one of the best players in the team took a shot and I saved it. That really changed my life at school. Everyone suddenly thought, he may be disabled, but he can play football!

I still had people making fun of my pink checked flares, but from that moment on, I loved school.

I didn't get into basketball until I was about 12 or 13 years old. There was a disabled school in the area, where they'd set up a sports club and within that a wheelchair basketball team called the Newham Rollers. At first, I didn't want to join. For a start, I didn't really think of myself as being disabled. Plus, I had a perception of wheelchairs as ugly, clunky things that said more about you than helped you.

But in the end, I went along and at the games I saw some of the guys from the GB basketball team, who happened to be training.

I was amazed by the chairs they were using – state-of-the-art funky wheelchairs – and they were flying up and down the court, doing wheelies and all sorts.

The players were all really big, with massive arms – they looked like athletes and were so cool.

As they were going past, one of them gave me a wink and I thought, that's it, that's what I want to be – I want to be like these guys.

I was getting frustrated at school playing football, because everyone else was getting bigger and it was harder and harder for me to compete with them, so I decided to try wheelchair basketball instead.

1985: I discovered wheelchair basketball.

1990: I was selected to try out for the Barcelona Olympics.

1995: I tried out for the Atlanta Paralympics.

2000: I took part in the Sydney Paralympics.

2004: I took part in the Athens Paralympics and won a bronze medal.

2005: I received an MBE.

2008: I commentated at the Beijing Paralympics.

2012: I commentated at the London Paralympics.

From *Balancing Act*

by Ali Sparkes

"Everyone," said Mrs Toynbee, as soon as they stepped inside. "I'd like you to welcome Lara Mitchell and Nicolai Cuvello." Around the brightly lit room, 28 faces turned to inspect the newcomers. There were murmurs of curiosity. "Nicolai prefers to be called Nico," went on Mrs Toynbee. "Nico – can you tell us a bit about yourself?"

Nico stared at his teacher in horror. Nobody had prepared him for this.

He put his bag down and stepped forward. And then did a back flip on to his hands and walked up and down with confidence and agility, his hair dangling towards the floor.

"Hi!" he said. "I'm Nico – known to many as Nugget the Clown. I've travelled the world with the Barry Smith Circus and been to about 20 different schools along the way. It's a nightmare to fit in, let me tell you! I'm really nervous – especially about the tall fair-haired boy and his mates who mistook me for a bouncy castle earlier. Really freaked out to find him right here in this class. And I can't even hope to move on soon and avoid him, because my parents have lost their minds and decided to buy a house!"

Except, of course, that's not what happened at all. Only in his head. In reality, he stood like a post and mumbled, "Um … I like gymnastics … and … comedy."

(A few days later, Nico was on a school trip when the minibus crashed, dangling precariously from a rocky ledge, held in place by a single cable. Nico knew he was the only one who could save them.)

There was only a light breeze as Nico stepped out on to the thickly woven wire. There was never a breeze in the Big Top, but he'd practised outdoors from time to time over the years, so he knew how it felt.

If he'd been surrounded by an audience, with a circus band playing and whoops and gasps of fear below, he would've felt fine. Excited and tense, yes, but fine.

But the circus high wire was about 15 metres across and about 6 metres up. This one was at least 40 metres across and too high to even think about. There was no band, no safety net and no audience, except five terrified people on a dangerously balanced minibus with an unconscious driver.

His heart raced so fast he could hear the blood pumping through his ears.

Focus, he told himself, his arms outstretched and steady. You can do this. Those people are depending on you.

_____

He ran, lightly and steadily, his agile toes and expert balance taking him across the valley like a spider on a line of silk. His hair blew back and he felt a rush of exhilaration almost obliterate his fear.

Don't look down, he warned himself. And don't get cocky!

Name:	Class:	Date:

> Questions 1–12 are about **Ade Adepitan: A Paralympian's Story**
> (pages 54–56).

1 How old was Ade when he contracted polio?

_____

1 mark

2 Why did his parents bring him to the UK?

_____

1 mark

3 Explain the phrase *all the memories came flooding back to me.*

_____

1 mark

4 Put ticks (✔) in the table to show which of these statements are **fact** and which are **opinion**.

	Fact	Opinion
Polio is contracted from polluted water.		
Nigerian trees are green and lush.		
Polio prevents muscle growth.		
The brown boots looked ugly.		

2 marks

5 Ade didn't like wearing his caliper and boot when he was young. Give **two** reasons why.

1. _____

2. _____

2 marks

6   **Find** and **copy** the word that means the same as 'machine-like'.

_____

1 mark

7   What do you think the other children thought of Ade when he arrived in the playground that first morning, and why?

Support your answer with reference to the text.

_____

_____

_____

2 marks

8   How old was Ade when he discovered basketball?

_____

1 mark

9   Give **two** reasons why Ade didn't want to join the Newham Rollers at first.

1. _____

_____

2. _____

_____

2 marks

10   **Find** and **copy** Ade's description of the wheelchairs used by the Newham Rollers and explain what it means.

_____

_____

2 marks

11 Which statement is the best summary for the **whole** text?

✓ Tick **one**.

Ade liked football and basketball. ☐

Ade learned to use a wheelchair. ☐

Ade overcame his disability to become a Paralympian. ☐

Ade contracted Polio when he was young. ☐

1 mark

12 What impression do you get of Ade Adepitan's character from reading his autobiography? Support your answer with evidence from the text.

_____

_____

_____

_____

_____

2 marks

Questions 13–20 are about *Balancing Act* (pages 57–58).

13 Why did Nico stare at his teacher in horror?

_____

_____

1 mark

14 *and walked up and down with confidence and agility*

Circle the word that has a similar meaning to *agility*.

ability   suppleness   carefulness   fear

1 mark

15 *he stood like a post and mumbled*

Why do you think Nico *didn't* say all the thoughts that were in his head?

_____

_____

1 mark

16 What advice did Nico give himself *before* he stepped onto the wire?

_____

1 mark

17 *he felt a rush of exhilaration almost obliterate his fear*

Explain the meaning of this sentence.

_____

_____

_____

1 mark

18 Nico was used to walking on the high wire in the circus, but the situation at the scene of the accident was very different.

Compare the two, giving evidence from the text.

In the circus	At the accident

3 marks

19 How does the character of Nico at the start of the text contrast with his character at the end? Justify your answer with reference to events in the text.

_____

_____

_____

2 marks

20 Ade Adepitan's autobiography and the story in *Balancing Act* share many similarities. **Summarise two** of them.

1. _____

_____

2. _____

_____

2 marks

Mark scheme for Autumn Half Term Test 1

Qu.	CD	Requirement	Mark
		The Weirdstone of Brisingamen	
1	2b	**Award 1 mark** for There is a station at Wilmslow, and **1 mark** for Susan and Colin are at the end of their journey.	2
2	2a	**Award 1 mark** for *debris*.	1
3	2d	**Award 1 mark** for answers linked to feelings of excitement, anxiety or being unrelaxed – not just that they are ready.	1
4	2b, 2d	**Award 1 mark** for the last miles, and **1 mark** for you are excited; you want to get there; you are waiting, not doing any other activities; you have no time to relax.	2
5	2a	**Award 1 mark** for crowds got off the train; poured off the train.	1
6	2b	**Award 2 marks** – **1 mark** for each piece of evidence from the text: e.g. *an oak of a man*; *solid as a crag*; *barrelled with flesh, bone, and muscles*.	2
7	2g	**Award 1 mark** for answers indicating he is round or curved – like a barrel.	1
8	2b, 2d	**Award 2 marks** for 4 correct answers; **award 1 mark** for 2–3 correct ticks; **award 0 marks** if all boxes are ticked: Mr Mossock was friendly – True; Mr Mossock was getting them some supper – False; Mr Mossock had a deep voice – False; Mr Mossock liked to be called Gowther – True.	2
9	2b, 2d	a) **Award 1 mark** for evidence, e.g. *eyed the children warily*. b) **Award 1 mark** for explanation, e.g. they were strangers; the dog had just woken up.	2
10	2c, 2d	**Award 2 marks** – **1 mark** for each piece of evidence from the text: No, not set in modern times: e.g. mackintosh; breeches; farm-cart and horse.	2
		Linnaeus: Organising Nature	
11	2b	**Award 1 mark** for all 3 correct adjectives: *important*; *influential*; *adventurous*.	1
12	2a	**Award 1 mark** for journey.	1
13	2b	**Award 1 mark** for in the northern parts of Sweden, Norway and Finland.	1
14	2d	**Award 1 mark** for to persuade the Royal Society of Uppsala to give him a grant.	1
15	2h	**Award 1 mark** for each view: mother was worried and hoped he wouldn't get the grant; father understood it was an important step in his son's career.	2
16	2b	**Award 1 mark** for 1732.	1
17	2b, 2c, 2h	**Award 2 marks** for all 8 correct ticks; **award 1 mark** for 4–7 correct ticks; **award 0 marks** if all boxes are ticked: 1732: a coat, second-hand leather breeches, a bag, a sword. Today: a coat, a mobile phone, a lightweight tent, a bag.	2
18	2d	**Award 1 mark** for cameras had not been invented.	1
19	2b	**Award 1 mark** for each correct piece of evidence from the text, e.g. followed herds of reindeer; lived in forests and mountains; lived on fish and reindeer; made clothes and tents from reindeer skin; healthy.	2
20	2c, 2d	**Award 1 mark** for an impression drawn from the whole text and **1 mark** for evidence, e.g. clever – most important scientist; adventurous/brave – went on expeditions to remote places; determined – persuaded Royal Society of Uppsala to give him a grant; curious – wanted to learn about the Sami.	2
		TOTAL MARKS	30

Mark scheme for Autumn Half Term Test 2

Qu.	CD	Requirement	Mark
		Hard Times: Growing up in the Victorian Age	
1	2b	**Award 1 mark** for 1901.	1
2	2a	**Award 1 mark** for *grand*.	1
3	2b	**Award 1 mark** for *made in large numbers by machines* (it must be the definition from the Glossary).	1
4	2b, 2d	**Award 1 mark** for 4 correct answers: Most rich children had a governess or tutor – True; Most children went to school – False; There were no boarding schools – False; Some poor children had to go out to work – True.	1
5	2a	**Award 1 mark** for accommodation; somewhere to live.	1
6	2b	**Award 1 mark** for 4 correct answers: 1842 – Females and boys under 10 were not allowed to work down the mines. 1870 – School Boards were allowed to set up new schools. 1880 – Attending school became compulsory for children aged between 5 and 10. 1891 – Education was made free and compulsory for all children.	1
7	2a	**Award 1 mark** for necessary; required; enforced; or a must.	1
8	2b	**Award 1 mark** for each correct answer: Girls – pinafores over their dresses; Boys – caps, trousers and jackets.	2
9	2b, 2d	**Award 2 marks** for 4 correct answers: **1 mark** for 2–3 correct answers Children sat in rows – Fact; Modern classrooms have bright displays – Opinion; Classrooms were lit by gaslight – Fact; Canes were used to punish pupils – Fact.	2
10	2b, 2c, 2d	**Accept either Yes** or **No** and **award 1 mark** (up to 3 marks) for each reason that is supported with evidence from the text, e.g. Yes – you didn't have to go to school; No – the teachers used canes.	3
		Nicholas Nickleby	
11	2b	**Award 1 mark** for *a month*.	1
12	2b	**Award 1 mark** for to give the boys brimstone and treacle.	1
13	2a	**Award 1 mark** for hunted; delved; looked through; searched.	1
14	2b	**Award 1 mark** for the reason and **1 mark** for evidence from the text, e.g. to save money – sulphur and treacle cost much less than breakfast and dinner.	2
15	2d, 2g	**Award 1 mark** for showing what the word means: claimed – like a belonging; owned; no one came forward to collect him. **Award 1 mark** for the hidden meaning, e.g. Smike has no family; Mr and Mrs Squeers make him work; it's not really kindness – it's free labour.	2
16	2a	**Award 1 mark** for it made him feel suddenly sad.	1
17	2b, 2d	**Award 1 mark** for an impression of what it was like and **1 mark** for evidence: Cold, dirty, dark, miserable, frightening – lacked most of its window panes; paper patches were all that blocked the cold.	2
18	2d	**Award 1 mark** for an opinion, e.g. cruel, mean, unkind, plus at least two references to evidence from the text for a further two marks.	3
19	2b, 2c	**Award 2 marks** for any relevant points from the text, e.g. cheaper than food; tasted horrible; sticky foul-smelling broth.	2
20	2c, 2d, 2e	**Award 1 mark** for **No** with evidence from the text, e.g. Mr Squeers was cruel; the boys were not looked after; no teaching; his heart sank at the situation.	1
		TOTAL	30

Mark scheme for Spring Half Term Test 1

Qu.	CD	Requirement	Mark
		All Things Beautiful – An Anthology of Poems	
1	2a	**Award 1 mark** for collection or series.	1
2	2b, 2d	Accept any insect that can be justified using the text and **award 1 mark** for each justification, e.g. Butterfly: colourful – *a burst of colour*, flutters – *a flit and a flutter*, flies – *flicker of wings*; floats gracefully – *dancing ballerina*.	2
3	2a	**Award 1 mark** for brief, quick, fast, speedy, passing or short-lived.	1
4	2b, 2d	**Award 1 mark** for busy; quick; rushing around; in a line; organised; disciplined – like soldiers. **Award 1 mark** for evidence from the text, e.g. *Hurrying, Scurrying, Marching, miniature army*.	2
5	2b, 2f, 2g, 2h	**Award 2 marks** for answers that show contrast, e.g. vocabulary – hurrying, scurrying vs. slipping, sliding; short one-word lines vs. long, smooth sentences.	2
6	2d	**Award 1 mark** for fox and accept any evidence from the text, e.g. *beady eyes*; *ruby coat*; *white-tipped tail*; *paws*; raiding the bins.	1
7	2d	**Award 1 mark** for any appropriate answer, e.g. the white tip of its tail is easier to see in the dark and might look like it's floating in the air.	1
8	2d, 2g	**Award 1 mark** for answer and **1 mark** for the justification from the text, e.g. dislikes it – word like *Squishy, slimy, Greasy*.	2
9	2d, 2g	**Award 1 mark** for an explanation e.g. because the petals are soft and delicate.	1
10	2b, 2c, 2d	**Award 2 marks** for answers that show a preference and make at least two references to the text.	2
		Coral Reefs	
11	2b	**Award 1 mark** for *a big underwater structure made of a stony substance called limestone* (must be a direct quotation).	1
12	2b	**Award 1 mark** for 2–3 correct answers and **2 marks** for 4 correct answers: All coral reefs like cold water – false; Most reefs are found in the tropics – true; Sunlight is important for coral reefs to grow – true; Water needs to be deep – false.	2
13	2a	**Award 1 mark** for circling both unusual and uncommon.	1
14	2b, 2c	**Award 2 marks** for including both pieces of information: in the Coral Sea, off the northeast coast of Australia.	2
15	2b	**Award 1 mark** for 3 correct answers: Red Coral Reef – location; near Israel, Egypt and Djibouti; New Caledonian Barrier Reef – Length: 1,500 km; Great Barrier Reef – Biggest reef on the planet.	1
16	2b	**Award 1 mark** for 4,265 years old.	1
17	2b, 2c	**Award 1 mark** for the correct order: 1 = Tiny baby corals float in the ocean; 2 = The polyps protect themselves with hard limestone; 3 = The polyps die and leave a little stone skeleton behind; 4 = Enough polyps grow and die to build up into a reef.	1
18	2b	**Award 1 mark** for each of 2 correct facts, e.g. body looks like a bag; opening for a mouth; have tentacles; polyps are nocturnal; 1–3 millimetres wide; live in colonies.	2
19	2b	**Award 1 mark** for *soil particles*.	1
20	2b, 2c, 2d	**Award 3 marks** for opinion evidenced with justification from the text, e.g. Agree: chemicals are killing coral; sediment is blocking sunlight; rubbish is killing creatures; turtles are eating plastic bags; fishing nets can tangle up on reefs and trap creatures.	3
		TOTAL	30

Mark scheme for Spring Half Term Test 2

Qu.	CD	Requirement	Mark
		Virginia Hall: World War II Spy	
1	2b	**Award 1 mark** for the better you can plan.	1
2	2a	**Award 1 mark** for *enemy*.	1
3	2b	**Award 1 mark** for each of 2 correct answers from the text, e.g. *How many people does the enemy have? What battle plans do they have? Who are their leaders?*	2
4	2d	**Award 1 mark** for 3 correct answers: Spies passed on top-secret information – Fact; Virginia Hall was a spy – Fact; Virginia Hall was one of the bravest spies – Opinion.	1
5	2d	**Award 1 mark** for an impression and **1 mark** for support from the text, e.g. they were brave – certain death if captured.	2
6	2a	**Award 1 mark** for important or necessary or crucial.	1
7	2a	**Award 1 mark** for *agents*.	1
8	2b, 2c	**Award 1 mark** for each of 2 correct answers, e.g. most information gathered by computers; information gathered from mobile phones; sophisticated listening stations; hacking into computers; monitoring texts and emails; CCTV and satellites.	2
9	2b, 2c, 2d	**Award 1 mark** for each supported reason, e.g. Yes – exciting; important work; No – dangerous; could be killed; no rewards.	2
		The End of the Line	
10	2d	**Award 1 mark** for because Ali kept saying the same thing over and over again.	1
11	2a	**Award 1 mark** for *(exasperated)*.	1
12	2b, 2c	**Award 1 mark** for the night before.	1
13	2c, 2d	**Award 1 mark** for each alternative answer with some reference to the text, e.g. excited – he wanted to go back; annoyed with Jed's behaviour – when he walks off; confused by Jed's behaviour – acting weird; curious to find out what Jed saw – Jed won't tell him.	2
14	2b	**Award 1 mark** for 2–3 correct answers and **2 marks** for 4 correct answers: Ali accused Jed of being scared – True; Jed wanted to go back to the factory – False; Jed admitted he was scared – False; Jed was white when he ran down the stairs – True.	2
15	2a	**Award 1 mark** for each of the following: *snoop* – look around, be nosy; *mannequin* – shop window dummy.	2
16	2d	**Award 2 marks** for an appropriate answer with justification from the text, e.g. she thinks it is funny; it has happened before; she thinks they will be friends again soon; she is 'teasing'; says 'Oh what's new!' and 'He'll be back in …'	2
17	2d	**Award 1 mark** for clothing.	1
18	2a, 2d	**Award 1 mark** for an explanation of the term and **award 1 mark** to explain why he looked at her in this way, e.g. a look of disdain; a dirty look; a sarcastic glare – because he thought she had said something silly.	2
19	2b	**Award 1 mark** for 4 correct answers: 1 = They found an unlocked door. 2 = They were playing with the mannequins. 3 = Jed went up the metal stairs. 4 = Jed was as white as a sheet.	1
20	2d	**Award 1 mark** for a plausible answer demonstrating that she was not really offended, and **1 mark** for evidence from the text, e.g. she pretended to be cross but wasn't really – she gave him *a playful push*; the phrase 'DO **NOT** even go there!' is usually used light-heartedly.	2
		TOTAL	30

Mark scheme for Summer Half Term Test 1

Qu.	CD	Requirement	Mark
		Daybreak	
1	2b	**Award 1 mark** for 12 years old.	1
2	2d	**Award 1 mark** for nervous, anxious or upset; **award 1 mark** for evidence to support this, e.g. her *fingers worrying at a loose button on her cardigan.*	2
3	2b	**Award 1 mark each** for *yell* and *fume.*	2
4	2b, 2d	**Award 1 mark** for an accurate explanation or a direct quotation – *a huge tidal wave of water piling down the estuary*; **award 1 mark** for Linnie thinks bores are very exciting and not boring.	2
5	2b, 2f	**Award 1 mark** for the vet is coming to the farm so they have to be there.	1
6	2b, 2c, 2f	**Award 1 mark** for previous spring's bore was a two-star, so much smaller bore; **award 1 mark** for this one is a five-star, so much more powerful bore.	2
7	2b	**Award 1 mark** for 4 correct answers: 1 = The family walked to a place on the river bank. 2 = A steep wave of water travelled down the river. 3 = Dad grabbed Linnie's arm. 4 = Everyone got soaked.	1
8	2b, 2c	**Award 1 mark** for each reason other than her birthday and five-star, e.g. the TV cameras were going to be there; hot dogs, ice-creams; surfers, canoeists, etc.	2
9	2b, 2f	**Award 1 mark** for 2 points and **2 marks** for all the points: to go to the field at dawn, without her parents knowing, and bring the cows up the farm, so they could go to the bore as planned.	2
10	2b	**Award 1 mark** for far corner of the field.	1
11	2d, 2g	**Award 1 mark** for because they were flowing rapidly down the hill.	1
12	2c, 2d	**Award 1 mark** for every 2 appropriate adjectives that show understanding of the text. Allow synonyms but no duplicates. her mother said they weren't going to the river – furious; she went to bed – upset; she saw the bore last spring – excited; she thinks of her new plan – confident; the cows begin to run towards the gate – frightened; the herd is stampeding down the lane towards the town – terrified.	3
		'Lost: One Nerve'	
13	2a	**Award 1 mark** for to lose confidence; become scared.	1
14	2d, 2g	**Award 1 mark** for it shows him on the inside and the outside: he wanted to be brave – but he failed at the last minute.	1
15	2d	**Award 1 mark** for reference to a school situation where the writer might be asked to speak in front of an audience – e.g. an assembly, school concert or performance.	1
16	2a	**Award 1 mark** for blocking the light or, more abstractly, making it appear dark by his presence.	1
17	2a	**Award 1 mark** for *anxieties.*	1
18	2b 2d	**Award 1 mark** for he just nodded, and **award 1 mark** for a plausible reason, e.g. he didn't want his dad to think he was being silly.	2
19	2b, 2d	**Award 1 mark** for he's lost his smile as well – he is unhappy.	1
20	2c, 2d	**a) Award 1 mark** for an appropriate 3-word summary – e.g. worried, nervous, scared. **b) Award 1 mark** for appropriate advice with reference to the text – stand up to the bully; talk to Miss Jones and tell her how you feel; tell your dad what has happened.	2
		TOTAL	**30**

Mark scheme for Summer Half Term Test 2

Qu.	CD	Requirement	Mark
		Ade Adepitan: A Paralympian's Story	
1	2b	**Award 1 mark** for 15 months old.	1
2	2b	**Award 1 mark** for they thought he would get better medical treatment.	1
3	2a	**Award 1 mark** for he began to remember lots of things.	1
4	2d, NC	**Award 1 mark** for every 2 correct answers: Polio is contracted from polluted water – Fact. Nigerian trees are green and lush – Opinion. Polio prevents muscle growth – Fact. The brown boots looked ugly – Opinion.	2
5	2b	**Award 1 mark** for each reason: they didn't look cool; they were uncomfortable.	2
6	2a	**Award 1 mark** for *robotic*.	1
7	2d	**Award 1 mark** for what other children may have thought and **1 mark** for evidence about why they thought this; accept answers that suggest the other children didn't like him or were wary of him because he was different, e.g. black; disabled; huge afro; pink flares; Nigerian accent.	2
8	2b	**Award 1 mark** for 12 or 13 years old.	1
9	2b	**Award 1 mark** for each point: he didn't think of himself as disabled; he thought wheelchairs were ugly, clunky things.	2
10	2a, 2b	**Award 1 mark** for the description and **1 mark** for the explanation: *state-of-the-art funky wheelchairs*; modern, trendy, cool, jazzy.	2
11	2c	**Award 1 mark** for Ade overcame his disability to become a Paralympian.	1
12	2d	**Award 1 mark** for each impression supported with evidence, e.g. accept answers that show an understanding of someone who has worked hard and persevered – was determined and strong minded; didn't let his disability get in the way – made the football team and represented his country at basketball.	2
		Balancing Act	
13	2b	**Award 1 mark** for because she asked him to introduce himself to the class and he wasn't prepared; he was nervous.	1
14	2a	**Award 1 mark** for suppleness.	1
15	2d	**Award 1 mark** for because he was nervous; he was embarrassed; he wasn't brave enough; he thought the other children would laugh.	1
16	2b	**Award 1 mark** for *Focus … You can do this.*	1
17	2a	**Award 1 mark** for he was so excited and happy, it helped him to overcome his fear.	1
18	2b, 2h	**Award 1 mark** for every 2 correct answers with references to the text that demonstrate the differences between being in the circus and being at the accident, e.g. In the circus, the wire was 15 metres across. At the accident it was 40 metres across. In the circus, there was a safety net. At the accident, there was a sheer drop. In the circus, there was no breeze. At the accident, there was a light breeze.	3
19	2d, 2f	**Award 1 mark** for a comparison, e.g. he was very shy and nervous at the beginning / he was brave at the end – a hero. **Award 1 mark** for reference to the text, e.g. he couldn't speak in front of the class / he saved the people in the minibus.	2
20	2c, 2f, 2h	**Award 1 mark** for each similarity and accept answers that reflect the fact they had both had a difficult time at their new school; they both felt they didn't fit in; both triumphed in the end.	2
		TOTAL	**30**

Name: Class:

Year 6 Reading Comprehension Record Sheet

Tests	Mark	Total marks	Key skills to target
Autumn Half Term Test 1			
Autumn Half Term Test 2			
Spring Half Term Test 1			
Spring Half Term Test 2			
Summer Half Term Test 1			
Summer Half Term Test 2			